EXPLORING CONCORD'S HISTORIC BURIAL GROUND:

SLEEPY HOLLOW CEMETERY

Includes Biographies of
Inspirational Nineteenth Century Citizens
Who Made Major Contributions to
Concord and to the World

This book was purchased at

THE OLD MANSE, CONCORD, MA (1769)

PUBLISHED BY
THE FRIENDS OF SLEEPY HOLLOW CEMETERY, INC.
CONCORD, MASSACHUSETTS

Copyright © 2018 by The Friends of Sleepy Hollow Cemetery, Inc.

All right reserved. This book may not be reproduced in whole or in part without written permission from the publisher, nor shall this book be reproduced, stored in a retrieval system, or transmited in any form or by an means, electronic, mechanical, photocopying, recording or other, without written permission from the publisher.

This book has been prepared and published by The Friends of Sleepy Hollow Cemetery, Inc. and was made possible through the generous contributions of donors who support the efforts of The Friends.

The Friends of Sleepy Hollow Cemetery are citizens who comprise a non-profit community organization with a mission to further enhance and promote the preservation, beautification, and appreciation of the public burial grounds of the Town of Concord.

ISBN - 978-1-5323-7965-9

Printed in the United States of America

The Friends of Sleepy Hollow Cemetery

P.O. BOX 313, CONCORD MA 01742-0313

info@friendsofsleepyhollow.org

www.friendsofsleepyhollow.org

Table of Contents

INTRODUCTION..7
MAP OF SLEEPY HOLLOW CEMETERY...............................8-9
A Hollow & Peaceful Retreat For "A Summer Twilight"..........11
The New Burying Ground..13
The Transformation of Sleepy Hollow to a Burial Ground......15
    Fairgrounds..18
    The Pines..18
    The Knoll..19
Sleepy Hollow's Civil War Marble Memories............................23
    Melvin Memorial...25
STORIES OF SOME OF THE NOTABLES...................................27
Artisits & Writers..29
    William Ellery Channing...29
    Katherine Kennicott Davis..30
    Edward Bliss Emerson...30
    Robert Bulkeley Emerson..30
    William Emerson..30
    Edward Waldo Emerson..31
    Mary Moody Emerson...31
    Daniel Chester French...33
    Sophia Peabody Hawthorne...34
    Harriet Mulford Lothrop...35
    Margaret Mulford Lothrop...36
    William Willder Wheildon..37
Civial War Era Activists and Abolitionists................................39
    Abigail May Alcott...39
    Ann Bigalow...40
    Mary Merrick Brooks..41
    Lidian Jackson Emerson...42

Table of Contents

    George Gray..42

    Ebenezer Rockwood Hoar..43

    George Frisbie Hoar...43

    John Shepard Keyes...44

    James Melvin..44

    George Lincoln Prescott...47

    Reverend Grindall Reynolds..47

    Franklin Sanborn...48

    Anna Maria Whiting...49

    William Whiting... 51

Progressive and Creative Contributors..53

    Anne Rainsford French Bush...53

    Ephraim Wales Bull..55

    Edward Carver Damon...57

    Charles Emerson..58

    Elizabeth Sherman Hoar...58

    William Henry Hunt...59

    Peter Hutchinson...59

    William Munroe...61

    Edward F. Nealey...61

    Elizabeth Palmer Peabody..62

    Minot Pratt...62

    Samuel Staples...63

    Sarah Alden Bradford Ripley... 64

    Mary Lemist Titcomb.. 65

    Harvey Wheeler.. 66

    Captain Artemas Wheeler..67

    William Wheeler... 67

ACKNOWLEDGEMENTS..69

PHOTO CREDITS..71

ORDER OF EXERCISES

—AT THE DEDICATION OF—

SLEEPY HOLLOW CEMETERY,

CONCORD, SEPT. 29, 1855, 2, P. M.

PRAYER, BY REV. B. FROST.

SINGING, BY THE AUDIENCE,

THE FOLLOWING ODE, WRITTEN FOR THE OCCASION,

BY F. B. SANBORN.   TUNE,--Brattle Street.

Shine kindly forth, September sun,
  From heavens calm and clear,
That no untimely cloud may run
  Before thy golden sphere,
To vex our simple rites to-day
  With one prophetic tear.

With steady voices let us raise
  The fitting psalm and prayer,—
Remembered grief of other days
  Breathes softening in the air;
Who knows not Death—who mourns no loss—
  He has with us no share.

To holy sorrow—solemn joy,
  We consecrate the place
Where soon shall sleep the maid and boy,
  The father and his race,
The mother with her tender babe,
  The venerable face.

These waving woods—these valleys low
  Between the tufted knolls,
Year after year shall dearer grow
  To many loving souls;
And flowers be sweeter here than blow
  Elsewhere between the poles.

For deathless Love and blessed Grief
  Shall guard these wooded aisles,
When either Autumn casts the leaf,
  Or blushing Summer smiles,
Or Winter whitens o'er the land,
  Or Spring the buds uncoils.

ADDRESS, BY R. W. EMERSON.

BENEDICTION, BY REV. L. H. ANGIER.

B. TOLMAN, PRINTER, CONCORD.

Broadside issued in 1855 announcing the dedication of Sleepy Hollow Cemetery.

Introduction

Sleepy Hollow Cemetery, located in Concord, Massachusetts — described by Ralph Waldo Emerson at its 1855 dedication as "happily divided by Nature as to admit the relation between the Past and the Present" — has a rich and fascinating history. The Cemetery serves as the final resting place of many of the authors that drove an American literary renaissance in the mid-1800's including Ralph Waldo Emerson, Henry David Thoreau, Nathaniel Hawthorne, Louisa May Alcott, Elizabeth Peabody and others. It is additionally a beautiful example of a "garden or rural cemetery" designed to respect the natural contours of the land and the preservation of the trees and plants.

While much has been written about the people buried in Sleepy Hollow Cemetery, the full history of the Cemetery itself has not been compiled into one story. The significance of this "quiet valley," (listed on the National Register of Historic Places) compelled The Friends of Sleepy Hollow Cemetery to create this history for the appreciation of visitors from around the world as well as for local citizens.

The Friends of Sleepy Hollow Cemetery are citizens who comprise a non-profit community organization with a mission to further enhance and promote the preservation, beautification, and appreciation of the public burial grounds of the Town of Concord.

Created in five distinct sections, Sleepy Hollow Cemetery today is considered one burying ground. With more information to follow about each section, the evolution includes:

- The New Burying Ground opened in 1823
- The first section referred to as Sleepy Hollow, opened in 1855
- The Fairgrounds, opened in 1869
- The Pines, opened in 1933
- The Knoll, opened in 1998

Sleepy Hollow Cemetery

CONCORD, MASSACHUSETTS

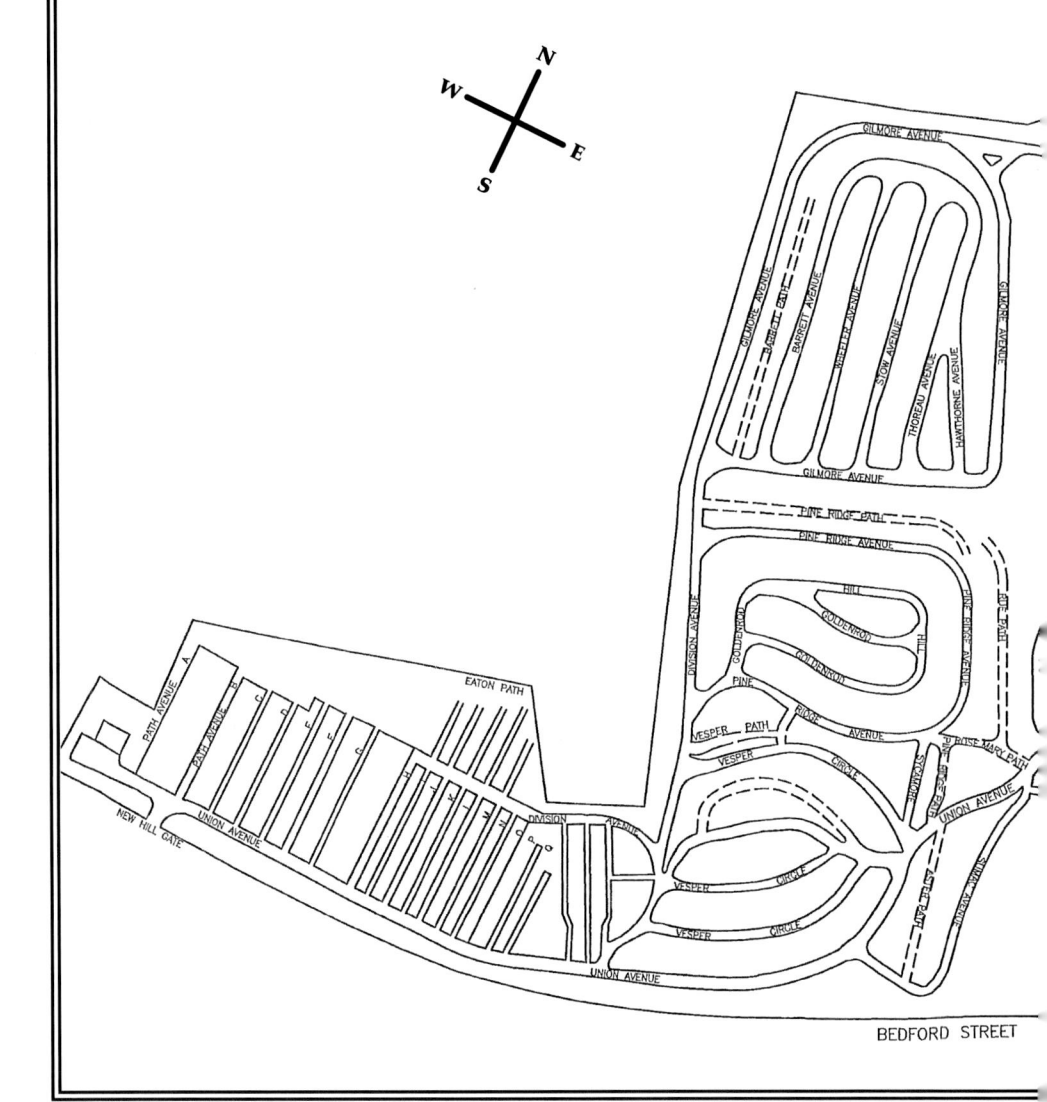

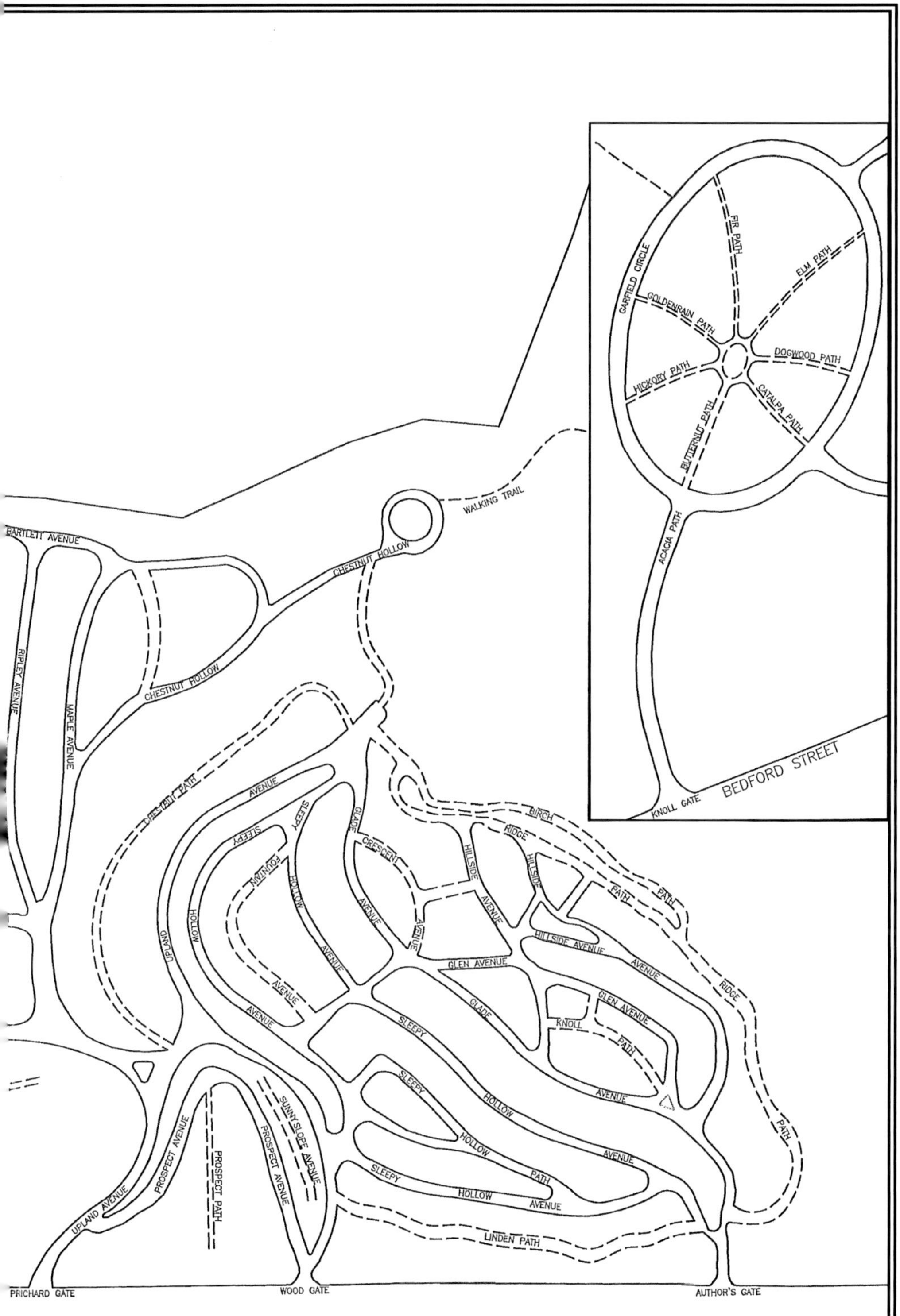
GARFIELD CIRCLE
FIR PATH
ELM PATH
GOLDENRAIN PATH
DOGWOOD PATH
HICKORY PATH
CATALPA PATH
BUTTERNUT PATH
ACACIA PATH
BEDFORD STREET
KNOLL GATE
WALKING TRAIL
BARTLETT AVENUE
CHESTNUT HOLLOW
CHESTNUT HOLLOW
RIPLEY AVENUE
MAPLE AVENUE
CHESTNUT PATH
AVENUE
SLEEPY
SLEEPY
FOUNTAIN
HOLLOW
GLADE
CRESCENT
AVENUE
AVENUE
HILLSIDE
AVENUE
BIRCH
RIDGE
HILLSIDE
PATH
PATH
HILLSIDE AVENUE
AVENUE
RIDGE
GLEN AVENUE
UPLAND
HOLLOW
AVENUE
AVENUE
AVENUE
GLADE
GLEN AVENUE
KNOLL
PATH
AVENUE
SLEEPY
SLEEPY
HOLLOW
AVENUE
PATH
HOLLOW
PATH
SLEEPY
HOLLOW
AVENUE
LINDEN PATH
SUNNYSLOPE AVENUE
PROSPECT AVENUE
PROSPECT PATH
PROSPECT AVENUE
UPLAND AVENUE
PRICHARD GATE
WOOD GATE
AUTHOR'S GATE

Nineteenth century view of a tree lined path in Sleepy Hollow Cemetery.

A Hollow

& PEACEFUL RETREAT FOR "A SUMMER TWILIGHT"

For 20 years before the Cemetery section known as Sleepy Hollow was dedicated, it was enjoyed by Concord writers as a favorite place to walk with nature, and to think and relax. With a natural amphitheatre or glacial hollow, Sleepy Hollow was called Sleepy Hollow even before it was a turned into a cemetery.

Nathaniel Hawthorne with his wife Sophia, Ralph Waldo Emerson, Margaret Fuller, Henry David Thoreau and others frequented this natural setting. Hawthorne wrote "I sat down in Sleepy Hollow…the present season a thriving field of Indian corn, now in its most perfect growth, and tasseled out, occupies nearly half the hollow; and it is like the lap of bounteous nature, filled with breadstuff." Hawthorne and Sophia planned to build their "castle" one day on the area now known as Authors Ridge and where Nathaniel and Sophia are interred.

Cannon from an 1812-era ship – restored by The Friends of Sleepy Hollow Cemetery – that serves as a memorial to Civil War veterans.

The New Burying Ground

With Concord's Old Hill and South Burying Place cemeteries filled, the Town of Concord in 1823 purchased a hilly plot and named it New Hill Cemetery. New Hill is fronted by a fieldstone wall that is topped with granite-block capstones. During one of the wall's repairs in the early 1870's, blocks from the dismantled 1789 jail – the same jail where Henry David Thoreau was imprisoned for not paying taxes – were installed as capstones with lines of notches for iron bars still evident.

New Hill or New Burying Ground is laid out with long rectangular blocks of graves divided by narrow paths, as was the fashion of the time period. Henry David Thoreau was originally buried in this section and later moved to Authors Ridge.

The New Burying Ground includes a small cannon from an 1812- era ship and serves as the Grand Army of the Republic (GAR) memorial for veterans of the Union Army, Navy and Marines who served in the Civil War

Sleepy Hollow Cemetery in the nineteenth century, highlighting the placement of graves along the paths.

The Transformation
OF SLEEPY HOLLOW TO A BURIAL GROUND

When it became apparent that Concord was running out of space again for burials of its citizens, John S. Keyes encouraged the town to purchase 25 acres of land from the estate of Reuben Brown. Ralph Waldo Emerson in his 1855 dedication of Sleepy Hollow Cemetery pointed out that the "seclusion from the village in its immediate neighborhood" made it ideal to be "given to the dead for the reaction of benefit on the living."

The Concord Cemetery Committee (of which Ralph Waldo Emerson was a member) hired Horace William Cleveland (H.W.S. Cleveland) and Robert Morris Copeland to design a burial ground that would respect the landscape and follow the contours of the land, creating an arboretum of native plants among the final resting places of Concord's dead.

The roughly 17-acre Sleepy Hollow section includes a steep path at the apex of the triangle leading down to Cat's Pond, an irregularly-shaped body of water. Henry David Thoreau – who surveyed and laid out the Pond – noticed that when completed in 1860, lilies and other plants were already growing in the pond and he reflected "in the midst of death we are in life."

Rather than a geometric grid of lots, Sleepy Hollow is a garden cemetery that places burial plots along paths and drives, and in Ralph Waldo Emerson's words, leaves untouched the "well disposed woods and waters, where art has been employed only to remove superfluities, and bring out the natural advantages."

At the consecration of Sleepy Hollow Cemetery on September 29, 1855, poet and Concord citizen William Ellery Channing wrote and delivered his dedication:

> *No abbey's gloom, nor dark cathedral stoops,*
> *No winding torches paint the midnight air;*
> *Here the green pines delight, the aspen droops*
> *Along the modest pathways, and those fair*
> *Pale asters of the season spread their plumes*
> *Around this field, fit garden for our tombs.*
>
> *And shalt though pause to hear some funeral-bell*
> *Slow stealing o'er the heart in this calm place,*
> *Not with a throb of pain, a feverish knell,*
> *But in its kind and supplicating grace,*
> *It says, Go, pilgrim, on thy march, be more*
> *Friend to the friendless than thou wast before;*
>
> *Learn from the loved one's rest serenity;*
> *To-morrow that soft bell for thee shall sound,*
> *And thou repose beneath the whispering tree,*
> *One tribute more to this submissive ground;*
> *Prison thy soul from malice, bar out pride,*
> *Nor these pale flowers nor this still field deride:*
>
> *Rather to those ascents of being turn*
> *Where a ne'er-setting illumes the year*
> *Eternal, and the incessant watch-fires burn*
> *Of unspent holiness and goodness clear,*
> *Forget man's littleness, deserve the best,*
> *God's mercy in thy thought and life confest*

Ralph Waldo Emerson in his address defends turning what was considered a retreat into a burial ground: "We must look forward… when these acorns, that are falling at our feet, are oaks overshadowing our children in a remote century, this mute green bank will be full of history: the good, the wise and great will have left their names and virtues on the trees: heroes, poets, beauties, sanctities, benefactors, will have made the air timeable and articulate." Speaking for himself and his friends and neighbors he commented, "In this quiet valley, as in the palm of Nature's hand, we shall sleep well when we have finished our day."

Teacher and abolitionist Franklin Sanborn's ode to Sleepy Hollow included:

> *These waving woods, these valleys low*
> *Between these tufted knolls,*
> *Year after year shall dearer grow*
> *To many loving souls;*
> *And flowers be sweeter here than blow*
> *Elsewhere between the poles*

With Sleepy Hollow Cemetery embraced by Concord's citizens, on April 19th, 1856, a tree-bee was organized and over a hundred trees were set out in a single day and recorded as a memorial to the person(s) who provided it.

Ralph Waldo Emerson is buried "under the pine-tree which he had chosen on the hill by the graves of his mother and child." Others of Concord's nineteenth century literary giants buried on Authors Ridge include Henry David Thoreau, Nathaniel Hawthorne, Louisa May Alcott and their families. As they were neighbors and friends in life, they are all buried in close proximity to each other.

THE FAIRGROUNDS

From 1855 until 1869 the area separating the New Hill Burying Ground from Sleepy Hollow was used as a fairground by the Middlesex County Agricultural Society. Annual cattle shows were held there starting in 1820 with indoor agricultural exhibits and competitions in the county courthouse. The grounds included a racetrack for horse racing, still outlined by the oval of Vesper Circle. It is reported that even today when new graves are dug in this area, layers of cinders from the racetrack are still found.

In 1869 the town annexed the section to expand the cemetery. The 100' x 40' exhibition hall was removed as well as cattle pens and livestock enclosures. Landscape designer Ernest Bowditch was hired to draw up plans but it is unclear if those plans were implemented.

The three sections – New Hill, Sleepy Hollow and the Fairgrounds – were linked by the 1870 construction of Union Avenue, even before the Fairgrounds section was laid out as a cemetery. Because the area was without vegetation, planting trees and evergreens became a priority. The Goldenrod Hill area of this section was developed by 1910 with a memorial flagpole, still in place.

THE PINES

In 1932 the Town of Concord purchased seven acres of land from the estate of Francis Gourgas, known as Gourgas Hill. This section is behind the former fairgrounds at the crest of a hill and was laid out with one encircling avenue. This section has been developed as a cemetery "park" with tall pine trees, ornamental shrubs and small-scale gravestones.

THE KNOLL

The Knoll is the most recent area developed for burials for Concord residents. This burying ground is about 25 acres and was originally farmland. In 1955, the land became available for sale and three Cemetery Committee members put down a deposit to hold the land so it could be voted at Town Meeting to be purchased for cemetery use.

This area is quite different from the gentle curves and rolling hills in the original part of Sleepy Hollow Cemetery. The land was originally known as Asparagus Farm and was owned by Enoch Garfield and his daughter Abbie Garfield Saunders who were related to President Garfield. The Knoll was designed with one circular road named Garfield Circle.

The Knoll is the first area of Sleepy Hollow to have a space designated specifically for religious burials. There is one section set aside for Jewish burials or others as long as they agree to abide by Jewish burial customs.

The original Prichard Gate entrance to Sleepy Hollow Cemetery.

The veterans of the First Massachusetts Heavy Artillery at the dedication of the Melvin Memorial, June 16, 1909.

21

Mourning Victory, from the Melvin Memorial.

Sleepy Hollow's
CIVIL WAR MARBLE MEMORIES

Six days following the April 12th, 1861, attack at Fort Sumter, George Buttrick, a newly minted soldier from Concord explained his decision to join the Union cause: "When the order came for me to join my unit, sir, I was plowing in the same field at Concord where my great-grandfather was plowing when the British fired on the Massachusetts men at Lexington. He did not wait a moment and I did not, sir." Among those who 'left the plow in the furrow" in response to the emergency, was George Buttrick, great-grandson of Major John Buttrick, who engaged British forces at the North Bridge in April, 1775. George is one of 157 Civil War veterans buried at Sleepy Hollow, many of whom are identified by "U.S. Civil War Veteran" markers.

The Concord Artillery, 5th Massachusetts Volunteer Militia, was the first unit from Concord to go to war in 1861, leaving town on a patriotic date that echoes 1775 – April 19th. On that day, 27-year-old Asa Melvin left the Hiram Jones farm on Westford Road, where he was employed as a farm hand and walked down Lowell Road into the center of town. Knowing that the Concord Artillery was preparing to head off to war, he desired to wish them well on their journey. Instead, upon hearing there was an opening on General George Prescott's roster, Asa enlisted on the spot. Without returning home to bid farewell to family members, or procure a change of clothes, he marched to the train depot with the company, beginning a journey that soon resulted in his unit's engagement at First Bull Run.

Asa was killed just before the Battle of Petersburg and buried by the side of the road. His brother Sam died at Andersonville Prison on September 25th, 1864, and is interred there in grave #9735. John Melvin was stricken with dysentery and succumbed to it at the Fort Albany Military Hospital in Virginia.

The Melvin Memorial.

THE MELVIN MEMORIAL

In 1897, James Melvin, the sole surviving Melvin brother, approached lifelong friend and Concord sculptor Daniel Chester French about commissioning a memorial as a tribute to his fallen brothers. The Melvin Memorial, "Mourning Victory," was finished in 1908, and consists of an image of "Victory" with her eyes downcast while clutching the American flag. The memorial is executed in Knoxville marble.

On June 16th, 1909, the forty-fifth anniversary of Asa's death, eighty-eight veterans of his regiment – the First Massachusetts Heavy Artillery – traveled in two special railroad cars to Concord from Boston for the Sleepy Hollow dedication ceremonies "standing in [the] silent camping-ground of the dead."

Upon the central shaft is inscribed:

> *In memory of three brothers born in Concord who*
> *As private soldiers gave their lives in the war to save the*
> *Country this memorial is placed here by their surviving*
> *brother, himself a private soldier in the same war.*

> *"I with uncovered head*
> *salute the sacred dead*
> *who went and who return not"*

26

Stories of
SOME NOTABLES BURIED IN SLEEPY HOLLOW CEMETERY

While much has been written about the numerous literary luminaries buried in Sleepy Hollow Cemetery— including Louisa May Alcott, Bronson Alcott, Ralph Waldo Emerson, Nathaniel Hawthorne and Henry David Thoreau — there are many other noteworthy contributors to American life who are buried in Sleepy Hollow Cemetery that deserve to be highlighted.

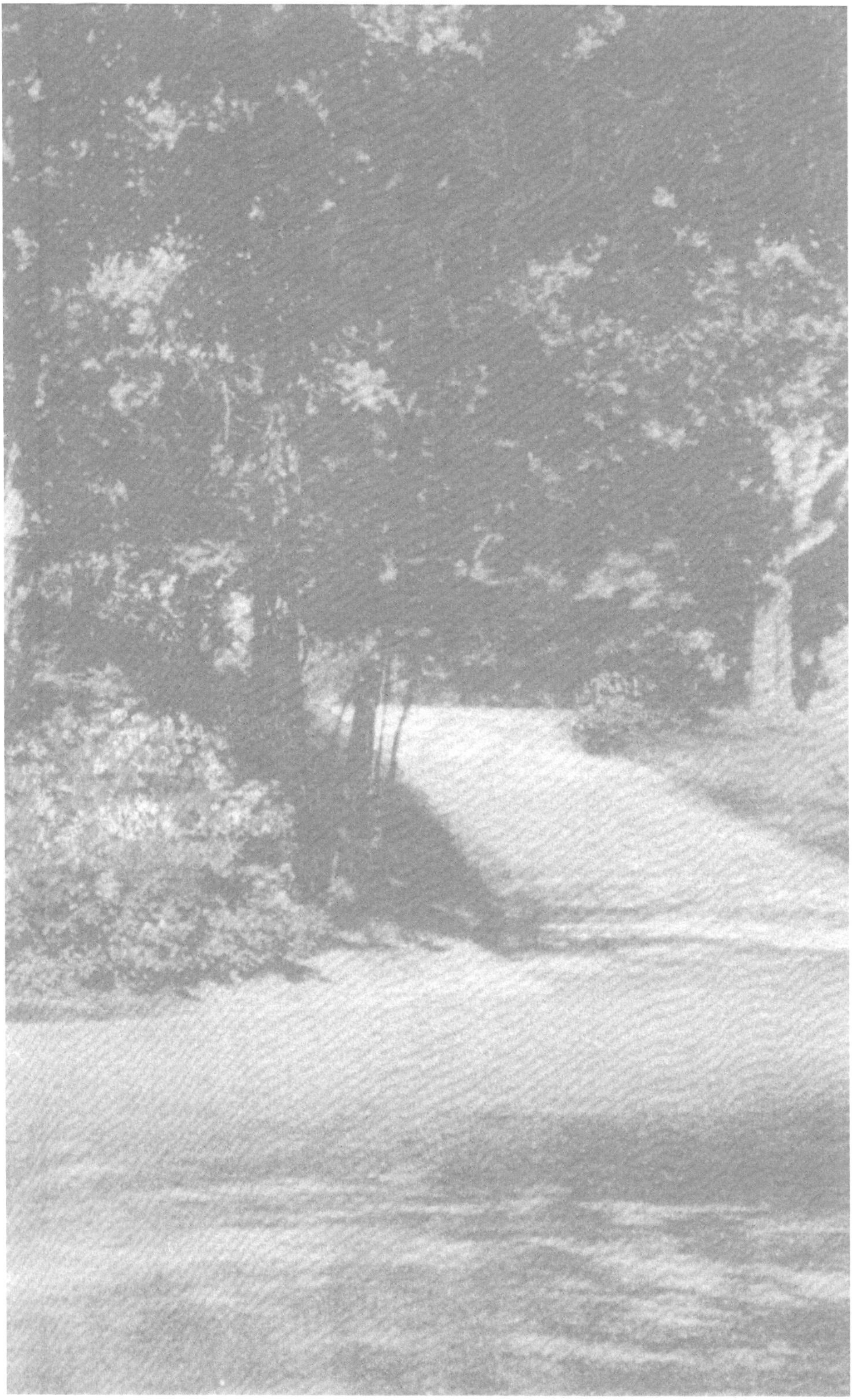

Artists and Writers

William Ellery Channing (1818 – 1901)

William Ellery Channing, the "younger" as he was known, was a transcendental poet and nephew of the Unitarian Minister, Dr. William Ellery Channing. In 1843, he published his first volume of poems re-printing them from the Transcendental magazine *The Dial*. He was a writer for the *Tribune* in New York City and from 1855 to 1856, was one of the editors of the *New Bedford Mercury*. Henry David Thoreau and Channing were frequent walking companions and he was a major influence on Thoreau. Channing once wrote a letter to Thoreau giving him this advice:" I see nothing for you on this earth but that field which I once christened 'Briars;' go out upon that, build yourself a hut, and there begin the grand process of devouring yourself alive. I see no alternative, no other hope for you". Thoreau soon embraced his advice and built his famous cabin next to Walden Pond. Channing was the first biographer of Thoreau and in 1873 published *Thoreau, the Poet-Naturalist*. Channing died on December 23, 1901 in Concord at the home of his friend Franklin Benjamin Sanborn, where he spent the last ten years of his life. **William Ellery Channing is buried on Authors Ridge.**

Katherine Kennicott Davis (1892 – 1980)

Katherine Kennicott Davis was a classical music composer with over 600 compositions. She was best known for the popular Christmas song, *The Little Drummer Boy* written in 1941. She composed her first musical piece, *Shadow March*, at the age of 15. She studied music at Wellesley College where in 1914 she won the college's Billings Prize. She also studied with Nadia Boulanger in Paris and completed graduate study at the New England Conservatory of Music in Boston. She was a music teacher at Wellesley College, Concord Academy in Concord, MA, and the Shady Hill School for Girls in Philadelphia. She left all of the royalties and proceeds from her compositions to Wellesley College's Music Department to help support musical instrument instruction. **Katherine Kennicott Davis is buried in The Pines section on Gilmore Avenue.**

The Emerson Brothers

Edward Bliss Emerson (1805 – 1834), Robert Bulkeley Emerson (1807 – 1859), and **William Emerson (1801 – 1868)** were three of Ralph Waldo Emerson's four brothers who survived to adulthood. William was the oldest son and with the early death of his father he helped to raise and support his younger brothers. After graduating from Harvard, he studied theology and philosophy at the University of Gottingen in Germany from 1824 to 1825. He eventually settled in New York City, where he practiced law and later served as a county court judge on Staten Island. William, Charles and Ralph Waldo kept up a continuous correspondence. **The brothers are buried with Ralph Waldo in the Emerson plot on Authors Ridge.**

Edward Waldo Emerson (1844 – 1930)

Edward Emerson was Ralph Waldo and Lidian Emerson's youngest child and is buried in a separate Emerson family plot as the one on Authors Ridge had run out of burial space. Edward became a physician with a busy practice in Concord and was an accomplished painter and author. Among other works, he authored a book about his father, *Emerson in Concord*, as well as a book about his one-time tutor Henry David Thoreau, *Henry Thoreau as Remembered by a Young Friend*. He was Superintendent of Schools in Concord, on the Board of Health and a member of the Cemetery and Library Committees. He additionally was a founding member of the Concord Antiquarian Society (now the Concord Museum).

Edward Waldo Emerson is buried in the second Emerson plot on Pine Ridge Path.

Mary Moody Emerson (1774 – 1863)

Mary Moody was Ralph Waldo Emerson's aunt, a prolific writer, reader, and religious seeker. When her brother William – Ralph Waldo's father – died at 42, she devoted herself to guiding, instructing and shaping her nephews' growth and development. Ralph Waldo Emerson was eternally grateful to his aunt who provided a function "which nothing else in his education could supply." In Robert Richardson's biography of Waldo Emerson *The Mind on Fire*, he writes that "Mary Moody's hunger for personal experience of the strongest, most direct kind must have pushed Waldo to settle for nothing less authentic, less direct, or less original in his own life." **Mary Moody Emerson is buried in the Emerson family plot on Authors Ridge.**

The Minuteman Statue – sculpted by Daniel Chester French in 1875 – located at the North Bridge.

Daniel Chester French (1850 – 1931)

Daniel Chester French was one of the most prolific and acclaimed American sculptors of the late nineteenth and early twentieth centuries and is best known for his design of the marble statue of Abraham Lincoln in the Lincoln Memorial in Washington, D.C. He studied anatomy with William Rimmer and drawing with William Morris Hunt. He spent a year at Massachusetts Institute of Technology as well as many years in Florence, Italy, in the studio of Thomas Ball. In 1872, he was commissioned by the Town of Concord to design the bronze Minuteman statue to be dedicated at the 100th anniversary of the Battle of the North Bridge.

In 1897, French was approached by his childhood friend James Melvin to create a memorial for Melvin's three brothers who died in the Civil War — Asa, John, and Samuel. The Melvin Memorial is called "Mourning Victory."

There is always an abundance of pennies on his gravestone left by visitors in the center of the wreath, Lincoln side up, in recognition of most famous work – the Lincoln Memorial.

His simple stone slab is decorated with a low relief sculptor that was designed by French himself. It depicts a laurel wreath with two sculpture tools attached at the base. Engraved on his gravestone below the wreath is his name, dates and a phrase that sums up his life's work: "A Heritage of Beauty." **Daniel Chester French's gravesite on Upland Avenue is appropriately right behind the Melvin Memorial.**

Sophia Peabody Hawthorne (1809 – 1871)

Sophia Peabody Hawthorne was an accomplished painter and illustrator having studied with Washington Allston and Thomas Doughty.

She married author Nathanial Hawthorne in 1842 and they began their lives together in Concord at The Old Manse. They had three children, Una, Julian and Rose.

When Nathaniel died in 1864 and was buried in Sleepy Hollow Cemetery, Sophia moved her family to Germany and later to England while pursuing educational opportunities for her children. She died in London in 1871 and was interred in Kensal Green Cemetery. In 1877, her daughter Una, who remained in London, died and was interred with her mother.

The other two children, Rose and Julian, returned to the United States, and Rose established a Catholic Order known as the Dominican Sisters of Hawthorne, dedicated to caring for cancer patients with no financial resources.

In 2006, almost 129 years later, the Sisters of Hawthorne wanted to bring Sophia and Una back to Concord, MA, to be buried with Nathaniel. With the consent of the Hawthorne descendants, the reinterment of Sophia and Una took place in Concord on June 26th, 2006. The town's horse drawn carriage hearse with two dapple grey percheron horses led the procession to the First Parish in Concord for memorial prayers, then processed to Sleepy Hollow Cemetery as family and friends followed by foot. A private family ceremony took place at the gravesite in Sleepy Hollow followed by a memorial service at the Old Manse in Concord, a place where the Hawthorne family lived as newlyweds. This reunion of the Hawthorne family at Authors Ridge is symbolic of the love that both Sophia and Nathaniel expressed so often in their letters and writings.

Sophia Peabody Hawthorne is buried on Authors Ridge.

Harriet Mulford Lothrop (1844 – 1924)

Harriet Mulford Lothrop wrote children's books under the pen name of Margaret Sidney. Her books were known as *The Pepper Books*. One of these books, *The Five Little Peppers and How They Grew*, sold over two million copies. She was married to Daniel Lothrop, a Boston book publisher, and they lived in The Wayside on Lexington Road and raised one daughter, Margaret Mulford Lothrop. A preservationist, Lothrop purchased and saved several historic homes in Concord including, The Grapevine Cottage, Ephraim Wales Bull's home on Lexington Road; The Wayside, the home where she lived and previously was the home of Nathaniel Hawthorne and the Alcotts; Orchard House, where *Little Women* was written by Louisa May Alcott; and The Thomas Pellet House, one of Concord's oldest homes located on Lexington Road. In 1895, she founded the National Society, Children of the American Revolution (CAR) and she delegated her daughter Margaret Lothrop as the first member. **Harriet Mulford Lothrop is buried on Authors Ridge.**

Harriett Lothrop, Elizabeth Peabody (sister-in-law of Nathaniel Hawthorne), Daniel Lothrop, and Margaret Lothrop (about 2 years old) at The Wayside, 1886-1887.

Margaret Mulford Lothrop (1884 – 1970)

Margaret Lothrop was the only child born to Daniel and Harriett Lothrop. She was born and grew up in The Wayside.

Lothrop graduated from Smith College and received her Masters from Stanford University. During WWI she was in the Red Cross where she was assigned as a Casualty Searcher in France to document graves, find families of men with memory loss, and speaking with dying men to identify their families.

Following in her mother's footsteps — Harriett Lothrop an active preservationist in Concord — Margaret saved The Wayside by opening it to tourists in 1928. She researched the occupants of the house and wrote *The Wayside: Home of Authors*. She had The Wayside declared a National Historic Landmark and sold the house to the National Park Service in 1965. **She was recently reinterred with her parents in Sleepy Hollow, and is buried on Ridge Path, across from the Emerson family plot.**

William Willder Wheildon – 1805 – 1892.

William Willder Wheildon was an historian, author and devoted member of the Bunker Hill Historic Association. A Massachusetts printer, newspaper publisher, editor, journalist, and writer of historical and literary topics, he wrote extensively about historic events in a publication he founded known as the *Bunker Hill Aurora* in Charlestown. The Bunker Hill monument was erected in Charlestown to commemorate one of the first major battles between the British and Patriot soldiers during the Revolutionary War.

Wheildon wrote predominately about the American Revolution. His various writings include *Memoir of Solomon Willard, Architect and Superintendent of the Bunker Hill Monument* and *A History of the Concord fight: Groton Minutemen at the North Bridge, April 19, 1775*. Moving from Charlestown to Concord in 1956 he was a member of many of Concord's historical and social organizations. **William Willder Wheildon is buried on Hillside Avenue and his unique family gravesite is bordered by 4 miniature replicas of the Bunker Hill Monument.**

William Willder Wheildon looking out from Nashawtuc Hill.

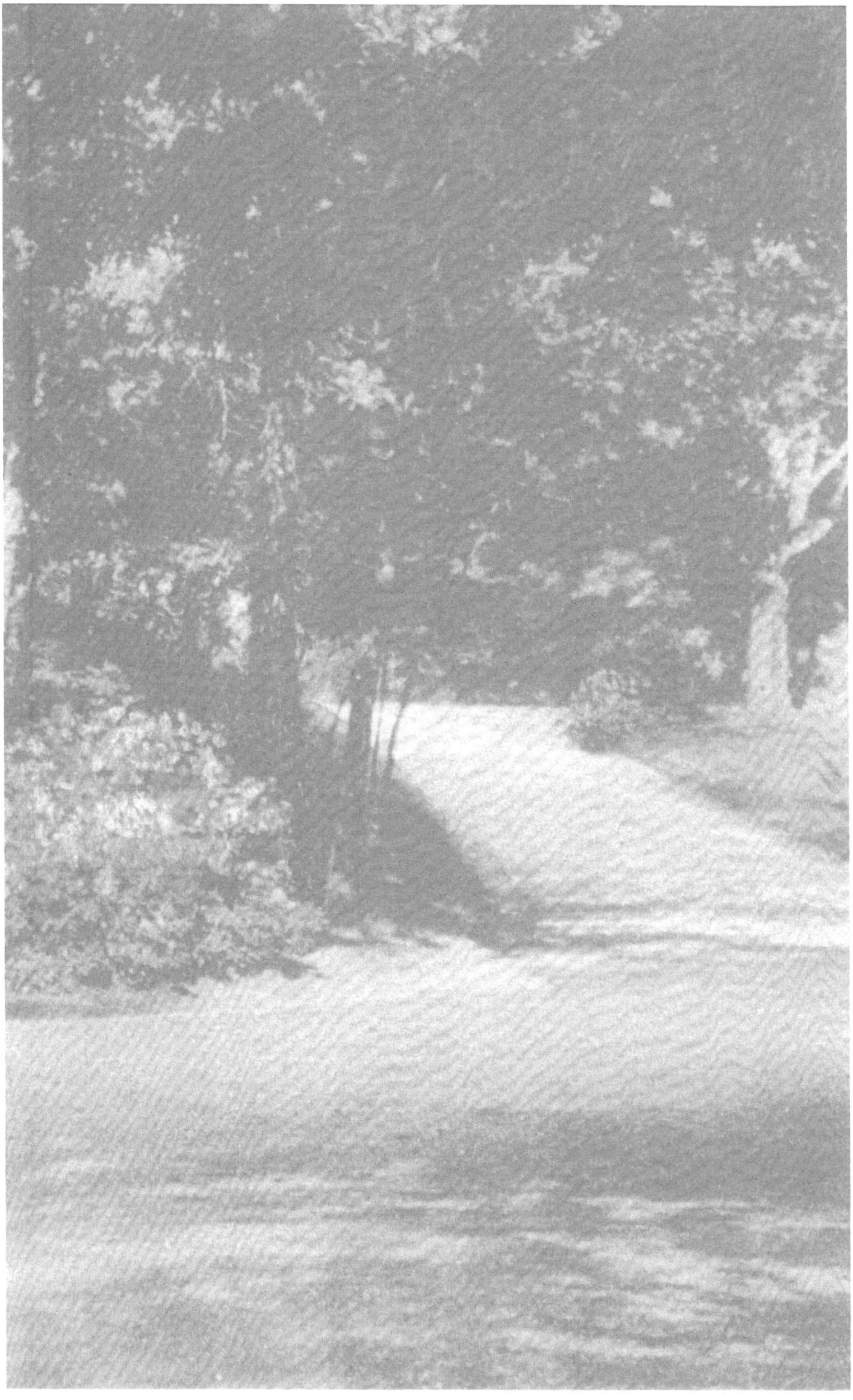

Civil War Era
ACTIVISTS AND ABOLITIONISTS

Abigail May Alcott (1800 – 1877)

Famous as the mother of author Louisa May Alcott, Abigail Alcott was an active woman in causes that included abolition of slavery, women's rights and pioneering social work. While her husband Bronson Alcott was one of the founding members of the first Boston anti-slavery organization, Alcott regularly attended abolitionist meetings and wrote in her journal, "Every woman with a feeling heart and thinking head is answerable to her God, if she do not plead the cause of the oppressed." She instilled her values for women to be active in social causes to her daughters, especially Louisa May Alcott, the author of the timeless classic *Little Women*. **Abigail May Alcott is buried with her family on Authors Ridge.**

Ann Bigelow (1813 – 1899)

Ann Bigelow and her husband Francis were active abolitionists with their home on Sudbury Road a critical part of the Underground Railroad, harboring fugitive slaves until they could be safely put on the train to Canada. One of the most famous rescues was the escape through Concord of Shadrach Minkins, a slave from Virginia working in Boston who was arrested and then "slipped away" by abolitionists. Shadrach was brought to the Bigelow's house at 3 o'clock in the morning and outfitted with clothes in preparation for his travel to Canada. Interestingly Mary Merrick Brooks' husband, Nathan, was a lawyer and legally bound to uphold the law, yet he too helped Minkins. **Ann and Francis Bigelow are buried on Knoll Path between Glen and Glade Avenues.**

Mary Merrick Brooks (1801 – 1868)

Mary Merrick Brooks—daughter of Concord storekeeper Tilly Merrick and wife of lawyer Nathan Brooks—was recognized during her life, and has since been celebrated, as a leader of the radical Concord Ladies' Antislavery Society. A founding member of the Society in 1837 and also a member of the Middlesex County Antislavery Society, Mary Brooks served as an officer for both organizations. A respected associate of abolitionists William Lloyd Garrison and Wendell Phillips, she uncompromisingly championed insistence on immediate abolition rather than gradual change through the political process. Her moral indignation over slavery was likely informed at least in part by the fact that, while living in South Carolina, her father had once been a plantation- and slave-owner.

> **Written for the Portland Transcript.**
> **BROOKS CAKE.**
>
> 1 pound flour, 1 pound sugar, half pound butter, 4 eggs, 1 cup milk, 1 teaspoonful soda, half teaspoonful cream of tartar, half pound currants (in half of it). This makes two loaves.
>
> The above cake has a history. In 1837 a woman's antislavery society was formed in Concord, Mass. Mrs. Brooks was president. Though a woman of property she desired to earn the money she used in the good cause, so she made cake by an unfailing recipe of her own, and sold it to her friends. It was named for her, and at every "tea-fight" in Concord, this cake was pretty sure to be found. A recipe which played such an important part in the antislavery movement is worth publishing for the benefit of the Transcript readers. We take it from "Warrington" Pen-portraits.   M. D. W.

Recipe for Mary Merrick Brooks "Brooks Cake" as it appeared in the Portland Transcript.

Mary Merrick Brooks was known for making and successfully selling a variety of pound cake —"Brooks Cake"— to raise money for the anti-slavery cause. The Concord Ladies' Antislavery Society meetings were held at members' homes. In 1857, the membership included Mrs. Brooks, Mrs. John Thoreau, Mrs. Minot Pratt, Mrs. R.W. Emerson, Mrs. E. R. Hoar, Mrs. Simon Brown, Mrs. Lucy Brown, Mrs. A.B. Alcott, Mrs. W.S. Robinson, Mary Rice, Sophia Thoreau, Ellen Emerson, and Martha Bartlett, among others.

Mary Brooks, along with Anna Marie Whiting, Ann Hager Bigelow and other women, beat off the deputies with their brooms as the deputies tried to arrest Franklin Sanborn on April 3rd, 1860. **Mary Merrick Brooks is buried with her family on Ridge Path.**

Lidian Jackson Emerson (1802 – 1892)

The wife of Ralph Waldo Emerson, Lidian Jackson Emerson was the mother of their four children, Waldo, Ellen, Edith and Edward and was, in the assessment of her daughter Ellen, as ardent about antislavery as her friend Mary Merrick Brooks. Like Mrs. Brooks, she was an active member of the Concord Ladies' Antislavery Society from its formation. She was a strong influence on her husband to move him to be more active in the cause against slavery. At her urging, on August 1st, 1844, in the Court House on Monument Square, Ralph Waldo Emerson delivered a powerful speech that placed him among effective public supporters of abolition. **Lidian Jackson Emerson is buried alongside her husband Ralph Waldo Emerson in the family plot on Authors Ridge.**

George Gray (1825 – 1901)

A carpenter and house builder, George Gray was attached to the 20th Massachusetts as a hospital steward, while his family resided in Concord. Writing in his *Memories of Concord Soldiers*, he described the engagement at Antietam in 1862, the most horrific day of combat in U.S. history, with 25,000 Union and Confederate dead, wounded and missing. Entire regiments were wiped out in minutes, "a desolate and appalling sight and brought sadness to the heart to contemplate the destruction of human life." Witness to the death of surgeon Edward Revere following this battle, he later described the death at Gettysburg of Edward's brother, Colonel Paul Revere. The brothers were grandsons of the "midnight rider" of Revolutionary War fame. Upon returning to Concord, Gray built a family home that became The Hawthorne Inn on Lexington Road. **Dying in 1901 at the age of 76, he is interred on Upland Avenue.**

Ebenezer Rockwood Hoar (1816 – 1895)

Ebenezer Rockwood Hoar had a lengthy and remarkable career in the U.S. judicial system. He served as Judge of the Massachusetts Court of Common Pleas from 1849 to 1855. From 1859 to 1869 he was Associate Justice of the Supreme Judicial Court of Massachusetts. President Ulysses S. Grant appointed him U.S. Attorney General in 1869, and Hoar later served as one of five members of the commission on Civil War claims against England, which resulted in the Treaty of Washington in 1871. He served a term in the U.S. House of Representatives from 1873 to 1874.

When deputies arrived in Concord on April 3rd, 1860, to arrest Franklin Sanborn, one of John Brown's Secret Six, Judge Hoar issued a writ in the middle of the night so that Sanborn could not legally be taken. **Judge Ebenezer Rockwood Hoar is buried in the Hoar family plot on Glen Avenue between Hillside Avenue and Crescent Avenue.**

George Frisbie Hoar (1826 – 1904)

Brother of Ebenezer Rockwood Hoar, George Frisbie Hoar served in the House of Representatives for three terms, and as a U.S. Senator from Massachusetts for five terms until his death. A strong fighter against political injustices, he campaigned for the African American and Native American rights, as well as being in favor of women's right to vote. He opposed the infamous Chinese Exclusion Act (forbidding Chinese immigrants to enter the U.S.).

Hoar was one of the founders of Worcester County Free Institute of Industrial Science, now known as the Worcester Polytechnic Institute. **George Frisbie Hoar is buried in the Hoar family plot on Glen Avenue between Hillside Avenue and Crescent Avenue.**

John Shepard Keyes – 1821 – 1910

John Shepard Keyes played very active roles during a vital period in Concord's history. He was elected sheriff in 1853 and, after serving as a delegate at the Republican convention that nominated Abraham Lincoln, he was made a U.S. marshal and was a bodyguard for Lincoln during his inauguration. Additionally he was present at Gettysburg when Lincoln delivered the Gettysburg address.

Keyes was a lawyer, a Massachusetts senator, a sheriff, U.S. marshal, and judge of the District Court. As Concord's Superintendent of Public Grounds, he was responsible for the purchase of the land that became Sleepy Hollow Cemetery. He wrote in his diary in 1855 "Thanks to me, we have a Sleepy Hollow Cemetery. I am quite content to take my long sleep in it and for my only epitaph, 'the Founder of this Cemetery.'" **John Shepard Keyes' grave is located on Birch Path.**

James Melvin (1848 – 1915)

James Melvin was the fourth Melvin brother to enlist in the Union Army and the only Melvin son to survive the Civil War. Following his return to Concord in 1864, he became a prominent Boston businessman and a principal figure in the development of the city's North End market district. In 1897, he commissioned sculptor Daniel Chester French to design the Melvin Memorial as a tribute to his three fallen brothers. This memorial, *Mourning Victory*, finished in 1908, consisted of an image of "Victory" with her eyes downcast while clutching the American flag. The tablet is a "salute to the sacred dead, who went and return not."

On June 16th, 1909, the forty-fifth anniversary of Asa Melvin's death, James Melvin hosted eighty-eight members of the 1st Massachusetts Heavy Artillery at the dedication ceremony where the Glee Club sang *Tenting To-night on the Old Camp Ground*, followed by a rendition of the *Battle Hymn of the Republic*. Melvin then feted the group at a luncheon in the main dining room of the Colonial Inn. **James Melvin is interred with his brother John in the family plot along Maple Avenue.**

WAR!
WAR! WAR!

The Freemen of Old Concord will meet

AT THE

TOWN HALL,

On Friday Evening, April 19th,

AT 7 1-2 O'CLOCK,

to take measures to fill up the ranks and strengthen the arms of

THE CONCORD ARTILLERY COMPANY,

that they may go forth to fight our country's battles as our fathers did in '75.

Come one! Come all!! From the farm and the workshop, the counting room and the office, and show by our action that we are not degenerate sons of brave sires.

CONCORD, April 17, 1861.

Broadside to gather volunteers for the Artillery Company to represent Concord in the Civil War.

THE PEOPLE OF CONCORD

ARE INVITED TO MEET AT THE

CHURCH OF THE FIRST PARISH,

—ON—

Wednesday, April 19th,

AT 12 O'CLOCK, AT NOON,

to unite in the solemnities to be observed by the whole country at the hour of the funeral of

ABRAHAM LINCOLN,

THE LATE PRESIDENT OF THE UNITED STATES.

And it is also requested that all labor and business be suspended on that day, between the hours of 11 and 2 o'clock.

NATHAN B. STOW, } Selectmen
ELIJAH WOOD, } of
BENJAMIN TOLMAN, } Concord.

CONCORD, April 18th, 1865.

Broadside announcing a memorial service at First Parish for recently assassinated President Abraham Lincoln. The service was held on the day of Lincoln's state funeral.

George Lincoln Prescott (1829 – 1864)

Civil War Union Brevet Brigadier General George Prescott was the owner of a lumber company next to the train depot in Concord and was commissioned as a colonel in the 32nd Massachusetts in December 1862. Following Bull Run, he took part in the battles at Fredericksburg, Chancellorsville, Gettysburg (where he was wounded), Cold Harbor and the Wilderness Campaign. In June, 1864, Colonel Prescott was mortally wounded near Petersburg while charging the enemy across an open field, succumbing to this wound the next day. Ralph Waldo Emerson referred to General Prescott's courage and compassion in Emerson's dedication speech for the Civil War obelisk in Monument Square on April 19th, 1867. **George Lincoln Prescott was later interred in a place of honor on what became Authors Ridge, laid to rest close to where Emerson, the Alcotts, Hawthorne and Thoreau are buried.**

Reverend Grindall Reynolds (1822 – 1894)

Serving thirty-six years as Minister of First Parish Church, Grindall Reynolds was actively engaged in the Concord Soldier's Aid Society during the Civil War. He packed boxes of foodstuffs and medical supplies while writing letters and knowing the stories of every Concord soldier off to war. On April 19th, 1865, four days following Lincoln's assassination, a town-wide memorial was held at First Parish, with Concord's Civil War veterans leading the processional. Mourners recognized this as a day never to be forgotten. The communion table, covered in black cloth, was placed in front of the sanctuary, below the steps leading to the pulpit. A basket of white flowers and a wreath of English violets prepared by Edith Emerson

(Ralph Waldo Emerson's daughter) were placed on top of the table. In front of the pulpit, shrouded in black, was a picture of Abraham Lincoln. Reverend Reynolds described the Lincoln assassination as "the blackest day in my memory, when we heard of the atrocious and meaningless murder of my great and good president."
Reverand Grindall Reynolds' grave is located on Chestnut Path.

Franklin Sanborn (1831 – 1917)

Franklin Sanborn was an ardent abolitionist and served as Secretary of the Massachusetts Free Soil Association and, as a zealous supporter of John Brown, joining forces with Theodore Parker, Samuel Gridley Howe, Thomas Wentworth Higginson, George Luther Stearns and Gerrit Smith – to comprise John Brown's "Secret Six." Sanborn also served as Superintendent of Public Charities for Massachusetts; was editor of the *Springfield Republican*; and one of the founders of the American Social Science Association.

On April 3rd, 1860, deputies tried to arrest Sanborn but neighbors prevented the arrest and Judge Rockwood Hoar issued the Writ of Habeas Corpus to make the arrest unlawful. Sanborn was committed to the custody of George Lincoln Prescott.

Franklin Sanborn was also a teacher who started his own coeducational school in Concord in 1855. His students included Ralph Waldo Emerson's children Ellen, Edith and Edward; Nathanial Hawthorne's son Julian; and Rockwood Hoar's son Sam.
Franklin Sanborn is buried along Chestnut Path.

Anna Maria Whiting (1814 – 1867)

Anna Maria Whiting, daughter of William Whiting, was a member of the Concord Ladies' Antislavery Society and wrote for the *Liberator* and *Herald of Freedom*. She and her sister Louisa Jane attended antislavery conventions and provided hospitality for visiting abolitionist lecturers. On June 8th, 1859, Frank Sanborn wrote Benjamin Smith Lyman regarding a visit by Harriet Tubman to Concord, "Miss Whiting took charge of her while here, and she [Tubman] spoke on Sunday night at a meeting in the vestry."

Anna Maria Whiting wrote a critical article for the September 27th, 1844 issue of the *Herald of Freedom* about the Concord Selectmen's refusal to ring the bell to announce the 1844 celebration of the Concord Ladies' Antislavery Society, (Henry Thoreau took care of the bell-ringing). She may also have been the person responsible for circulating the 1849 Concord petition on behalf of Washington Goode, a free Boston black man arrested in 1848 for murder and sentenced to death.

In 1860, when federal officials attempted to arrest Franklin Sanborn in Concord for his involvement with John Brown, Anna Maria Whiting did her fearless best to obstruct their efforts. Ellen Emerson wrote her sister Edith on April 4th, 1860, that "Miss Anne Whiting got into the carriage and held the door and put herself in the way, and fought with a cane, and so prevented them from getting Mr. Sanborn in… The men hurt her and scratched her and tore her dress trying to get her out, but she stayed in and hindered them a long time." Louisa May Alcott wrote, "Sanborn was nearly kidnapped. Great ferment in town. Annie Whiting immortalized herself by getting into the kidnapper's carriage so that they could not put the long legged martyr in." **Anna Maria Whiting is buried with her family on Authors Ridge.**

Mary Brooks along with Anna Marie Whiting, Ann Hager Bigelow and other women, beat off the deputies with their brooms as the deputies tried to arrest Franklin Sanborn on April 3, 1860.

William Whiting (1788 – 1862)

Colonel William Whiting (a carriage maker) and his wife Hannah Conant Whiting raised their family in Concord. Whiting was involved in antislavery at the local, county, and state levels. He gave liberally, for his means, to the anti-slavery cause. William Lloyd Garrison, Wendell Phillips, and John Brown, were guests at his house, and he subscribed, with other people of Concord, to aid John Brown in his operations in support of freedom in Kansas. He sheltered runaway slaves, and helped them on their way; and concealed Franklin Sanborn in his house, when Sanborn was hiding from an expected arrest by authority of the United States Senate for refusing to testify on the subject of Brown's invasion of Virginia.

Whiting was a member of the Boston Vigilance Committee. Judge Rockwood Hoar declared that Whiting's "best wish for his country was gratified by the proclamation of President Lincoln abolishing slavery, which just preceded his (Whiting's) death." **William Whiting is buried in the family plot on Authors Ridge.**

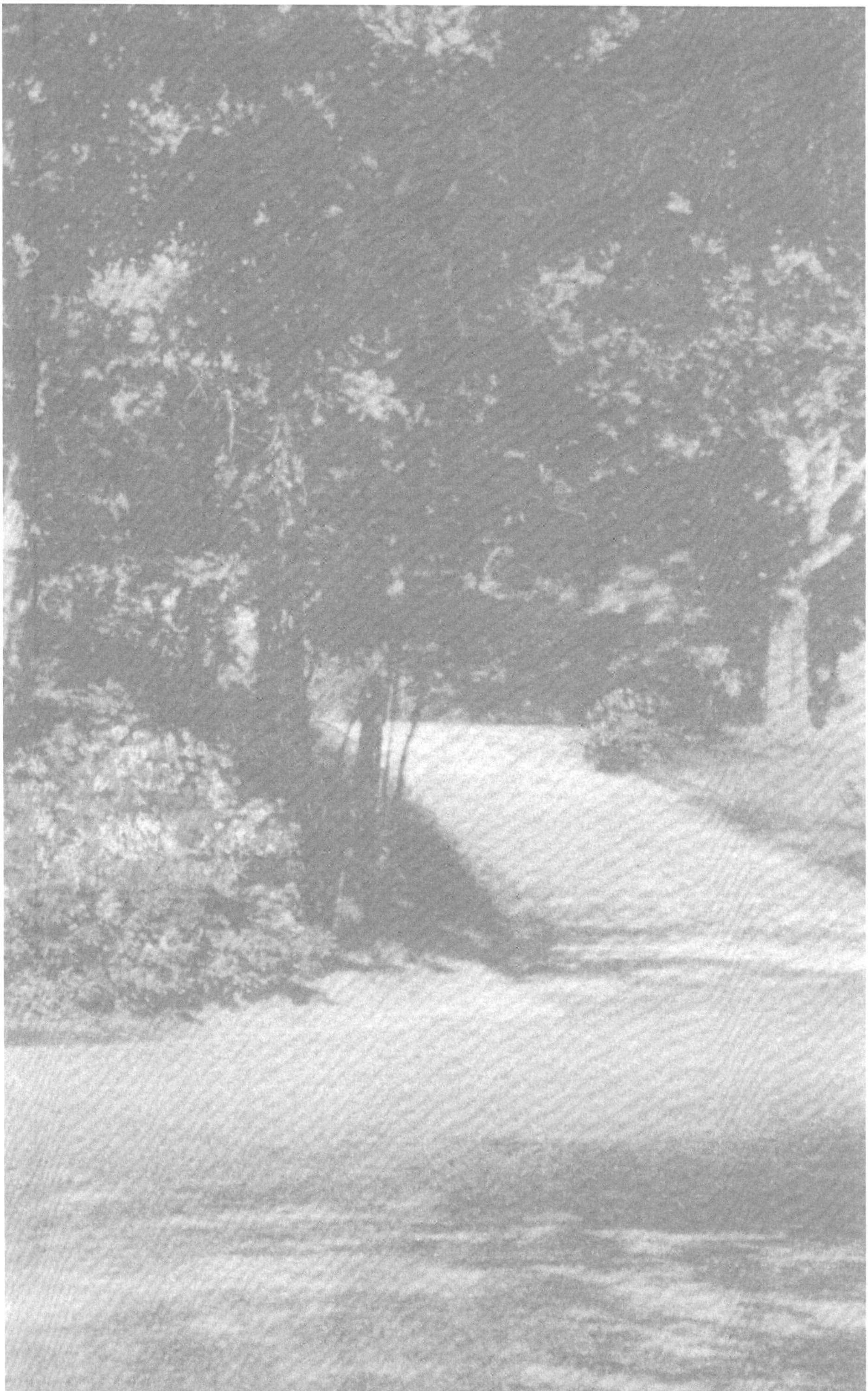

Progressive and
CREATIVE CONTRIBUTORS

In addition to the artists, writers and Civil War activists and abolitionists already mentioned, there are others buried in Sleepy Hollow Cemetery who contributed to society in important and unique ways.

Anne Rainsford French Bush (1878 – 1962)

On March 22nd, 1900, Anne Rainsford French Bush, niece of sculptor, Daniel Chester French and his wife Mary French, received a steam engineer's license, issued by the City of Washington, D.C. The daughter of a physician, she helped her father clean his steam powered locomobile. He told her if she did well he would let her drive the car. She did and received a steam engineer's license, entitling her to operate a four wheeled vehicle powered by steam or gas. When Anne married Walter Bush, they settled in Concord and she quit driving all together, taking up the traditional role of homemaker. Several years later the Automobile Club of American invited Anne to participate in their 50th anniversary celebration in Washington, D.C. While there, she had tea with Bess Truman and then fulfilled what Anne said was "a life-long dream," she drove a fire engine up Pennsylvania Avenue. **Anne Rainsford French Bush's gravestone on Vesper Circle reads: "First Woman Licensed to Drive an Automobile in America."**

Ephraim Wales Bull with his Concord grapevine.

Ephraim Wales Bull (1806 – 1895)

Ephraim Wales Bull was born in Boston and worked as a goldsmith. Due to poor health he was advised to leave the city and move to the country. He soon purchased a farm on Lexington Road in Concord where he could pursue his passion for horticulture. For many years he cultivated over 22,000 grape seedlings, and in 1849 his hard work paid off with his discovery of the Concord grape. He died penniless because cultivators were able to duplicate his seedlings from the vines he sold for five dollars each. His gravestone, a large boulder with a bronze plaque, reads: "He sowed, while others reaped." This quote could have two meanings: first, that many people were able to reap the monetary benefits from his discovery, or second: that many people reaped the benefits of the delicious taste of the grape. Either way Bull's legacy will be long remembered since his grape is used today for making many varieties of wine, jelly, juice and candy. **Ephriam Wales Bull's grave is located on Glen Avenue, just below Authors Ridge.**

The Damon Mill in the early 1860's.

Edward Carver Damon (1836 – 1901)

Edward Carver Damon succeeded his father in running the Damon Mill in West Concord. His father had created a domett cloth in high demand for Union soldier uniforms during the Civil War. He changed the face of what is now known as West Concord, with a neighborhood growing up around the mill providing housing, schools and a store for the workers.

He built and diversified the business, and served as a director of the Middlesex Institution for Savings, the Concord National Bank, eventually becoming Concord National Bank's president. He worked tirelessly with William Munroe to create the Concord Free Public Library, and served as a Selectman, School Committee member, and Water Commissioner. **Edward Carver Damon is buried on Ridge Path on Authors Ridge.**

Charles Emerson (1841 – 1916)

Charles Emerson was the son of Ralph Waldo Emerson's older brother William. He graduated from Harvard College, served in the Civil War, and then settled in Concord. After his wife died in 1910, he gave the New England Deaconess Association 40 acres of land in Concord and money to build the Concord Hospital. Later renamed Emerson Hospital — after Charles Emerson — the hospital was designed to enable patients who could not afford to pay to receive care for free and those that could afford it to pay. **Charles Emerson and his wife Theresa are buried in the Emerson family plot on Authors Ridge**

Elizabeth Sherman Hoar (1814 – 1878)

Elizabeth Sherman Hoar was engaged to marry Charles Chauncy Emerson in 1836 (the brother of Ralph Waldo Emerson) but Charles died of tuberculosis prior to the wedding. An ardent transcendentalist, "Aunt Lizzie" was a constant figure in the Emerson family. She was part of Emerson's Transcendental circle and helped with the *Dial* magazine, becoming friends with Margaret Fuller, Sarah Alden Bradford Ripley, the Alcotts and Elizabeth Peabody. Elizabeth Hoar often assisted in the running of the Emerson household during Lidian Emerson's illnesses. A childhood friend of Henry David Thoreau, she helped him prepare the garden at the Old Manse as a wedding present for Nathaniel Hawthorne and his bride Sophia Peabody. **Elizabeth Sherman Hoar is buried in the Hoar family plot on Glen Avenue between Hillside Avenue and Crescent Avenue.**

William Henry Hunt (1839 – 1926)

William Henry Hunt was a Concord farmer with his family farm located on Punkatasset Hill, Monument Street. He was the brother of Martha Hunt whose drowning was captured by Nathaniel Hawthorne in *Blithedale Romance*.

Hunt was a member of the Horticultural Society of Boston, Overseer of the Poor and member of the School Committee. He donated the money to build Hunt Gym (still in Concord) and was a member of the Social Circle in Concord from 1882. He wrote *Reminiscences of the Old Hunt House on Monument Street* providing an insight into life in Concord and antislavery feelings with his family. **William Henry Hunt is buried on Chestnut Path.**

Peter Hutchinson (1799 – 1882)

Peter Hutchinson was an African-American citizen of Concord. He was well known in town for his skills as a woodcutter, fisherman and sheep shearer. Ralph Waldo Emerson referred to Hutchinson in his poem, "Peter's Field" and Thoreau referred to Peter as a "dextrous pig butcher." John Shepard Keyes recalled that Peter "had more local knowledge of wood lots and meadow bounds than any man in town, and much of it died with him". According to Thoreau's Journals, places in Concord were named in tribute to Hutchinson: Peter's Path, a cart path that connected Monument Street to Peter's home on Bedford Street; Peter's Spring, a natural spring located near the filter beds of the Great Meadows area of Concord; and Peter's Field, a field located in the Great Meadows. **Peter Hutchinson's gravesite located on Union Avenue in the New Hill Burying Ground of Sleepy Hollow was un-marked for over 130 years. In 2013, The Friends of Sleepy Hollow Cemetery and the Robbins House teamed up to mark his gravesite.**

The Concord Free Public Library, which opened in 1873.

The gravesite of William Munroe, who was the founder of the Concord Free Public Library. The Friends of Sleepy Hollow Cemetery are responsible for restoring the fence.

William Munroe (1806 – 1877)

Raised in Concord, William Munroe, Jr. was a successful businessman in the dry goods business, working in London and Boston, amassing considerable wealth.

Although intensely focused on his career, Munroe maintained a deep and abiding affection for Concord. In the Social Circle memoir of William it was written, "He was proud of its [Concord's] history and the memorable events which took place here, and, more than all, of the illustrious men who claimed Concord as their home, whose words and deeds have had such a potent influence in shaping the history of the Commonwealth and nation."

Munroe, after retirement, summered in Concord in his family's home at the corner of Main Street and Academy Lane. Munroe, almost single handedly, took on the creation and establishment of the Concord Free Public Library, surmounting numerous obstacles. He purchased private property, moved buildings, widened Main Street, negotiated and made arrangements with the Town of Concord, Middlesex County, and the Commonwealth, encouraged the generosity of others, oversaw the move of the Town Library collection into the new building, and, in the last months of his life, planned the eventual expansion of the new facility. **The Munroe family plot is bordered by a black iron fence that was restored by The Friends of Sleepy Hollow Cemetery and is located on Hillside Avenue.**

Edward F. Nealey (1835 – 1909)

Edward F. Nealey was a wheelwright born December 2nd, 1835, in Wayland, MA. A friend of Henry David Thoreau, they took frequent walks together through the woods of Concord. In a Thoreau Society publication *Thoreau's Gait* by Brent Ranalli, Edward Nealey is quoted as saying, "he always walked with easy long steps; it would tire me well to keep up with him."

On one of these walks, Edward and Henry found a large Indian mortar stone, and Edward told Henry he wanted it to be used for his (Nealy's) gravestone. **This Indian artifact is situated along Union Avenue often used as a natural birdbath and engraved:** *Edward F. Nealey, 1835 – 1909.*

Elizabeth Palmer Peabody (1804 – 1894)

Elizabeth Palmer Peabody was born in Billerica, MA on May 16th, 1804. She was the sister of Sophia Hawthorne, (wife of author Nathaniel Hawthorne) and Mary Peabody Mann, (wife of educator Horace Mann). Choosing not to marry, Elizabeth Peabody was a Transcendentalist, writer and publisher, opening a bookstore at her home in Boston where she published books for Nathaniel Hawthorne, the Transcendental magazine *The Dial* and others. In 1860, she helped to establish kindergartens in America. She believed early childhood education was important for children under the age of six to learn cleanliness, manners, and have an understanding of numbers and shapes. As an early teacher at Bronson Alcott's school — the Temple School — in Boston, she believed that children's play was an integral part of learning. **Elizabeth Palmer Peabody's gravestone is located on Upland Avenue and reads: "*A Teacher of three generations of Children and the founder of Kindergartens in America. Every humane cause had her sympathy and many her active aid.*"**

Minot Pratt (1805 – 1878)

Minot Pratt was born and raised in Weymouth, MA. In 1829 he married Maria Jones Bridge and a young clergyman, Ralph Waldo Emerson, performed the ceremony (his first). Pratt was a printer and poet. His contact with Emerson, Unitarian Minister George Ripley and William Ellery Channing had a large impact on his view of nature and spirituality. He and his family were early participants in Brook Farm, the embodiment of an ideal community started by George Ripley.

At Brook Farm, Pratt discovered his intense interest in wild plants. After the Brook Farm experience, the Pratts moved to Concord a few months before Thoreau moved to Walden Pond. Pratt became a farmer and cultivator. He was also chosen as Secretary pro-tem for the Middlesex Anti-Slavery Society. He became very good friends with Thoreau due to their deep interest in wild plants. Pratt recorded his plantings, many from other areas of New England. Pratt authored a manuscript *Plants of Concord*, given to the Town of Concord.

The Pratt's son John Bridge Pratt married Anna Alcott, Louisa May Alcott's older sister. **Minot Pratt is buried on Ridge Path on Authors Ridge.**

Samuel Staples (1813 – 1895)

In July of 1846, Sam Staples, the town Constable, arrested and jailed Henry David Thoreau for not paying his poll tax for six years. Thoreau was opposed to the tax revenues being used to support the enforcement of slavery laws and the Mexican War. Sam himself offered to pay Henry's tax, but Henry refused. It is not known who paid the tax later that evening, but when Sam asked Henry to leave, Henry was outraged and refused to leave since he had not paid the tax himself. Sam Staples insisted and based on that experience, Henry wrote one of his most powerful essays, *Civil Disobedience*. Three years earlier, Sam had arrested Bronson Alcott for not paying his taxes. Although arrested, he was never jailed. Squire Samuel Hoar, the town's leading citizen, paid Alcott's taxes to avoid the Alcott family embarrassment. **Sam Staples is buried on lower Hillside Avenue.**

Sarah Alden Bradford Ripley (1793 – 1867)

On October 6th, 1818, Sarah married Samuel Ripley, the son of Ezra Ripley, Minister of First Parish in Concord, and Phebe Bliss (Emerson) Ripley. A noted scholar, Sarah Ripley was conversant in many languages as well as mathematics, chemistry, astronomy and botany. She easily could have filled any faculty chair at Harvard and in fact she ended up tutoring "rusticated" Harvard students. Her personal quest for continuing education was challenged by the births of her seven children. She wrote even though she had been "moved by influences from without to give up the independence of an attic covered with books for the responsibilities and perplexities of a parish and a family," she commented that she had "enjoyed much and learned more."

She was a close friend of Mary Moody Emerson (Ralph Waldo Emerson's aunt). Additionally, she assisted her husband in running a boarding school in Waltham to prepare boys for Harvard before she and her husband retired to The Old Manse (Samuel inherited the Manse) where she continued to learn and lived for 20 years. **Sarah Alden Bradford Ripley is buried between Ridge and Birch Paths.**

An early bookmobile, a service started by Mary Lemist Titcomb to bring books to citizens in rural counties.

Mary Lemist Titcomb (1852–1932)

Mary Titcomb was born in New Hampshire and, after deciding to be a librarian as her chosen career, apprenticed at the Concord Public Library. Her brother George Eugene Titcomb was a physician in Concord.

Eventually Mary Titcomb moved to the Washington County Free Library in Maryland, where the books were not accessible to citizens of rural communities without libraries nearby. Seeing this need, Titcomb set up deposit stations around rural communities, which then developed into an idea of a bookmobile.

Mary Titcomb launched the bookmobile, or "book wagon" service in 1905, delivering books with a horse-drawn wagon and bringing a wealth of knowledge through books to those who otherwise would not have access. Driven to improve library services, she also instituted library-training classes for her library personnel, which continued until 1931. **Mary Titcomb is interred in the family plot above Upland Avenue and near Daniel Chester French's grave.**

Harvey Wheeler (1847 – 1917)

Harvey Wheeler, for whom the Harvey Wheeler Community Center in West Concord is named, was a prominent citizen who was president of the Boston Harness Company, located in West Concord, filling extensive orders during the Civil War. Wheeler was Chairman of the Board of Selectmen and served three terms in the Massachusetts House of Representatives. He also served as president of the Middlesex Institution for Savings in Concord and was a member of Concord's Social Club.

Wheeler was generous to his workmen as well as using his wealth in the advancement of Concord public institutions. Upon his death it was voted to inscribe his name on the newly built school building in West Concord, now the Community Center. **Harvey Wheeler is buried on Chestnut Path**.

Captain Artemas Wheeler (1781 – 1845)

Captain Artemas Wheeler was a gunsmith in Concord. He served as a Captain in the War of 1812. In 1818, he was granted a patent for a rotating cylinder that fired five or more chambers before reloading. It was the precursor to the Colt revolver. His white marble gravestone standing tall is engraved: *Sacred -To the memory of -Capt. Artemas Wheeler -who died January 11, 1845 -Age 64 -Sudden from wife and children torn -The tender father hence was born -At night in health he closed his eyes -But slept in death, no more to rise -Then learn the living from the dead -How easy breaks life's tender thread.*
Captain Artemas Wheeler is buried on Union Avenue

William Wheeler (1851 – 1932)

William Wheeler was a civil engineer and educator who first brought fresh drinking water to Concord homes. An early graduate of Massachusetts Agricultural College, Wheeler worked as a civil engineer until William Clark Smith, the President of MAC, was asked by the Japanese government to help establish an agricultural college in Hokkaido, bringing Western technology and ideas to the new venture. Clark asked Wheeler to join him and while in Japan he taught mathematics, civil engineering and English as well as taking on projects, including the Sapporo Clock Tower, still there today. Wheeler succeeded Clark as President of the new college and remained in Japan until 1879.

Upon returning home, among other town contributions, he designed Concord's first waterworks, including the first sewage treatment plant. **William Wheeler is buried on Birch Path.**

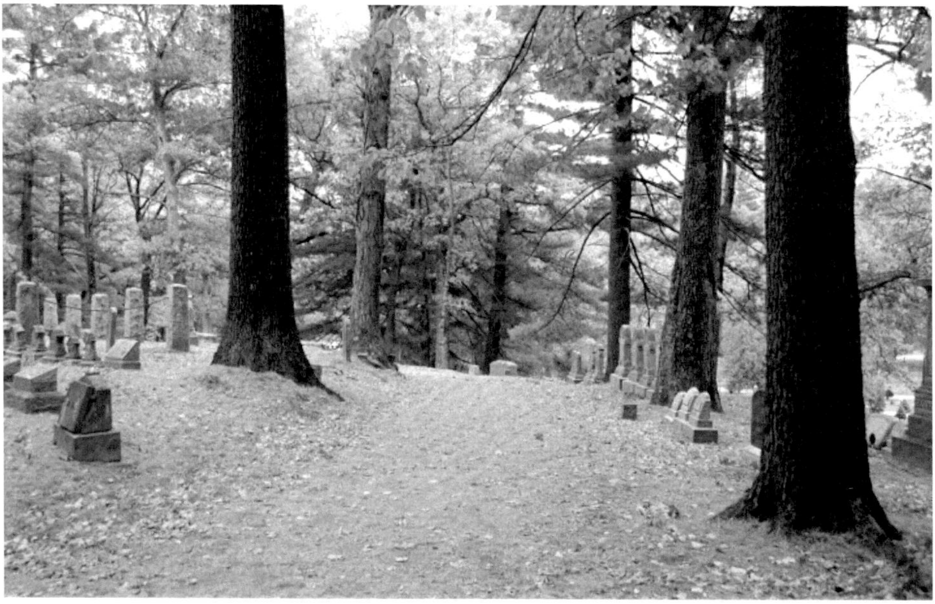

Acknowledgements

The Board of Directors of The Friends of Sleepy Hollow Cemetery, Incorporated, wholeheartedly supports and endorses appreciatively the preparation and publishing of this Guide to Sleepy Hollow Cemetery. Special gratitude is extended with distinction and pleasure to the Directors who researched, wrote, designed, and edited the welcome publication: Susan Dee, Barbara Ewen, Rick Frese and Priscilla White Sturges. Their quality work merits the highest commendation for its content and presentation. Please enjoy!

This Guide would not have been possible without the help and support of many people and Concord resources including Anne Forbes, Jayne Gordon, Patricia Hopkins, Conni Manoli, Leslie Wilson, the Concord Free Public Library and the Dee Funeral Home.

Kevin Thomas Plodzik, Ed.D.
President
Board of Directors
The Friends of Sleepy Hollow Cemetery, Inc.
Concord, Massachusetts 01742

July, 2018

Photo Credits:

Front cover: Postcard courtesy of Rick Frese. **Page 6:** Courtesy of Special Collections of the Concord Free Public Library. **Page 10:** Postcard courtesy of Tish Hopkins. **Page 12:** Photo by Priscilla White Sturges. **Page 14:** Postcard courtesy of Susan Dee. **Page 19:** Courtesy of Special Collections of the Concord Free Public Library. **Page 20-21:** Courtesy of Special Collections of the Concord Free Public Library. **Page 22:** Courtesy of Special Collections of the Concord Free Public Library. **Page 24:** Photo by Priscilla White Sturges. **Page 26:** Courtesy of Special Collections of the Concord Free Public Library and Courtesy of the Minute Man National Historical Park. **Page 29:** Courtesy of Special Collections of the Concord Free Public Library. **Page 31:** Courtesy of Special Collections of the Concord Free Public Library. **Page 32:** Postcard courtesy of Barbara Ewen. **Page 33:** Courtesy of Special Collections of the Concord Free Public Library. **Page 34:** Courtesy of Special Collections of the Concord Free Public Library. **Page 35:** Courtesy of Special Collections of the Concord Free Public Library. **Page 36:** Courtesy of Minute Man National Historical Park. **Page 37:** Courtesy of Special Collections of the Concord Free Public Library. **Page 39:** Courtesy of Special Collections of the Concord Free Public Library. **Page 40:** Courtesy of Special Collections of the Concord Free Public Library. **Page 41:** Courtesy of Special Collections of the Concord Free Public Library. **Page 42:** Courtesy of Special Collections of the Concord Free Public Library. **Page 43:** Courtesy of Special Collections of the Concord Free Public Library. **Page 44:** Courtesy of Special Collections of the Concord Free Public Library. **Page 45:** Courtesy of Special Collections of the Concord Free Public Library. **Page 46:** Courtesy of Special Collections of the Concord Free Public Library. **Page 47:** Courtesy of Special Collections of the Concord Free Public Library. **Page 48:** Courtesy of Special Collections of the Concord Free Public Library. **Page 50:** Courtesy of Special Collections of the Concord Free Public Library. **Page 54:** Courtesy of Special Collections of the Concord Free Public Library. **Page 56:** Courtesy of Special Collections of the Concord Free Public Library. **Page 57:** Courtesy of Special Collections of the Concord Free Public Library. **Page 58:** Courtesy of Special Collections of the Concord Free Public Library. **Page 60:** *(top)* Courtesy of Special Collections of the Concord Free Public Library and *(bottom)* photo by Priscilla White Sturges. **Page 62:** Courtesy of Special Collections of the Concord Free Public Library. **Page 65:** Courtesy of the Washington County Free Public Library, Maryland. **Page 66:** Courtesy of Special Collections of the Concord Free Public Library. **Page 68:** Photo by Priscilla White Sturges.